THINGS
I Didn't Think
I Thought

David Senften

ISBN 978-1-64492-853-0 (paperback)
ISBN 978-1-64492-854-7 (digital)

Christian Faith Publishing, Inc.
832 Park Avenue
Meadville, PA 16335
www.christianfaithpublishing.com

Printed in the United States of America

What people are saying about
Things I Didn't Think I Thought

I just finished your writing. Thank you for sharing it. You are courageous to be so open. After reading your work, I am thinking, *What do I believe, and why?* I am amazed that scripture can be so personal. Our God is truly wonderful.

—Mindy

I was not prepared to explain my spiritual beliefs in a clear and concise manner—even to myself. If you are like me, a person who longs for clarity in their beliefs, this book can be of great value. It provides a template that anyone can use on a spiritual journey that will bring clarity to their beliefs.

—Ed

I found this short book to be very readable and quite thought provoking. I especially like the part dealing with where we are after we die. Many of the questions you explore have been much on my mind. I think many people—Christians and non- Christians alike—will appreciate your effort to encourage others to sort out their thoughts and beliefs on extremely complex subjects.

—Phyliss

This is a must-read for anyone who thinks of themselves as a questioner, not only in the realm of spirituality, but also in any area of our lives where we can't put words to why we feel the way we do. It made me question some of my own beliefs that I felt confident in the origins of, as well as encouraged me to open my mind to the possibility that there may just be things that are impossible to prove beyond a doubt, but that doesn't mean that they can't still be a guide in our lives. I loved that complex topics were broken down in more simplistic terms that even a layperson like myself could understand and that they were presented without a feeling of judgment or superiority. I truly enjoyed reading these words, and they inspired me to continue to explore my thoughts at a deeper level.

—Amanda

*Now faith
is the substance
of things hoped for,
The evidence of things not seen.*

—Hebrews 11:1

FOREWORD

When I was about thirty-five years old, I met a man named Dave, who was in his mid-sixties. He was a successful businessman and inventor with a charming personality, and we quickly became friends. One of the things that made a lasting impression on me was his humility. This is a man of great wisdom and experience, yet when I interact with him, I feel like his peer. There is a gentleness about him that I very much wish to emulate. That spawned an idea. Have you ever heard the saying "You are the average of the five people you spend the most time with"? I believe this to be true, and I have paid attention over the past several years as the five people in my life change, as to how it makes me feel. One day it occurred to me that I could "manage my average" by deliberately selecting the five people I spend the most time with. I decided to invite Dave to be one of my five.

We began meeting biweekly about three years ago, and thus spending several hours together each month simply "thinking and talking about God." We had no syllabus or agenda, simply an open discussion. We soon began to learn that often the most thought-provoking conversations came when we would ask ourselves some difficult questions about what we believe: Does God ever change his mind? Is the devil real? Is he eternal? Does evil come from sin, or is sin caused by evil?

What we found was that one or two questions like this provided a springboard for discussions that have challenged us to explore what we truly believe (not just what we say we believe).

Then one day, as leaders will do, Dave began to lead us to something new. As we explored our beliefs together, he began capturing his solidifying understandings of his beliefs and the thinking that got him there, by committing them to paper. The result is the book that you are about to enjoy. This book doesn't teach you what to think, but it might very well help you learn how to think more meaningfully about what you believe.

Praise God for our spiritual companions in this life. My life has been forever impacted by this exploration of my true personal beliefs, and by my friendship with Dave. So I ask you this: what do you believe?

Larry Lund
Spiritual Companion

ACKNOWLEDGMENTS

I believe that no one writes alone.

Even if we were completely isolated from all other living creatures, we are in the company of our memories, our hopes, our fears, our beliefs, our dreams, and our God. I have been more than fortunate to have had all these persistent companions and a bunch of very much alive human spiritual companions with me throughout the journey of this writing.

My friends Larry and Ed and my wife, Connie, gave essential help in pushing back the darkness of uncertainty and unknowing, allowing beliefs to spring into being. They, along with other friends and acquaintances, encouraged and supported my efforts along the way. All that way, I was never alone. To all these staunch companions who have made the journey with me, I am much indebted and offer my most sincere gratitude.

"You hold me by my right hand. You guide me with your counsel" (Psalm73:23–24).

Thanks to each of you who have held my hand with your support and illuminated the way with your insightful and loving counsel.

Introduction

Most Americans (68 percent) believe that God or another intelligent force created us. But a study by Jonathan P. Hill, PhD, of Calvin College, sponsored by the BioLogos Foundation, went on to say that the harder you press about historical claims in the Bible, the less confident people are. Of that original 68 percent, less than half (30 percent) would say that they were absolutely certain that God was directly involved in creation. The survey went on to say that 37 percent believed that God created the world in six 24-hour days. Others said it took Him billions of years. Others said He wasn't involved at all. Thirty-six percent said humans came into existence within the last ten thousand years; still others said, No, it was more like two hundred thousand years ago. How is anyone supposed to know what to believe?

So what do you believe?

There are a lot of things that I say I believe. But do I really?

I suspect that a good many of the things I say I believe are ideas or concepts that I have picked up from other sources that sounded good or comforting to me at the time, so I tucked them away in my belief system without considering whether they would stand up under some thoughtful scrutiny.

Can you produce a clear statement of your beliefs?

I couldn't.

What you will find as you read this book is a journey of discovery that I hope could be a template by which you would construct a journey of discovery of your own. A journey that could change matters of faith that you hope to be true into reasoned beliefs. It has for me. I believe it could do the same for you.

Do you have doubts and questions that have been with you for a long time?

I do.

Finding clarity in my spiritual beliefs has helped me resolve gnawing doubts and questions that I have carried since childhood. This has been a great benefit in my overall spiritual growth.

Without that clarity, my witness of faith has been lacking in substance.

———— ••• ————

What started as an investigation of a specific spiritual question, undertaken by a seeker brought up in the Christian tradition, evolved into a broad-scoped spiritual quest. As you would expect, the conclusions reached were arrived at through the lens of that culture. But I believe that an experience of this type could be of great value to anyone regardless of their spiritual heritage. A journey you might take, in your own way, based on your background, would almost certainly be different and would bring you to different conclusions along the way. That's the beauty of it. We are all defined by the unique relationship that each of us has with God. And it is incumbent upon us to continue to love those whose beliefs are different than our own in ways that respect and honor one another's personal relationship with God.

As you read this book, you will find that portions of it are written in different fonts. Some portions will be the words spoken directly to the reader. Those will be (presented in this font). There will also be portions where the words are words that capture the essence of thoughts and ruminations that emanate from the struggle of the journey. Those words will be **(presented in this font)**.

PREFACE

In a conversation not all that long ago, I mentioned to a counselor that often when I experienced a spiritual aha moment, it brought tears to my eyes. At the end of our conversation together, my counselor said, "You might want to think about why you have tears when you experience those aha moments."

So I did. After some thought, I determined that it happened when something caused an element of my spiritual belief system to go from "I hope this is true" to "I believe this is true." The tears accompanied the feeling of relief as I released a hope that I had been clutching tightly and was able to replace it with a firm belief that allowed me to say, "I know, I *know*."

Rarely had I ever intentionally stopped to consider what I really believe. But then something happened. There was a strange series of events that led me to take a more critical look at what I say

I believe and why I believe it. And it seemed like maybe I should write it down.

———————

In May of 2017, I was hard at work in my home electronics lab. The lab was crowded with workbenches and equipment, more so than usual as I had just added a new project. I was feeling pressed to complete this particular project because it was an important element of my fishing navigation and steering system, and the best fishing season was upon me. As often happens to me, a new project had pushed the previous "new" project back on the workbenches, which had pushed the previous, previous "new" project even farther back, until on this day, I had five unfinished projects spread over every square inch of workbench space and another in the basement. My wife will tell you that for all of our married life, much of my spare time has been consumed by my passion for some kind of design/build project to the point that she has felt at times like an electronics widow.

This day was no different. I had been drawn irresistibly into my lab and this hot new project. I had three power supplies, two oscilloscopes, and a voltmeter all hooked up and doing their thing. It was electronics heaven.

I had immersed myself in this wonderfully stimulating environment for several hours when I decided to take a break. I turned off the power supplies and other equipment and left everything hooked up so that I could pick up right where I left off when I came back. As I write this, it is eleven days until Christmas. Everything on my work-benches is exactly as I left it seven months ago. In all that time, I have had no compulsion to go back to work on those projects. That is not like me at all.

It took a while, but eventually it struck me and my wife, Connie, that something had hap-pened. This was not what either of us would have expected. I think it would have been totally appro-priate if Connie would have said, "You're not the man I married," and been happy about it. For me, it did not feel scary or unsettling, but there was a sense of expectancy. This change in me had not been a decision that I had made. Something else had to be going on. I waited.

I began filling my time with music, playing, listening, a little composing and then one morning I was reading through the Twenty-third Psalm just for the solace that it gives me, and when I came to the word *evil*, I just stopped. What do I know about evil? I mean, nobody talks about evil much. My parents, and even the pastors I've had over the years, kind of shied away from the subject. Oh yes, they told me there is evil, and to stay away from it. They would say something like, "Beware of the devil. Be good, or he or his demons will gitcha."

But, what is evil? Where did it come from? When did it get here? Is there really an evil entity, the devil? Are sin and evil the same thing? Is all sin evil? Is all sin evil inspired? I wondered. The questions intrigued me, so I decided to investigate, starting with scripture and going from there. I began to research and write down what I found so that I could remember it. Here is where it led me.

EVIL

Genesis tells us that God created the universe and everything in it in six days, and it was good. There was no evil. Evil came to humanity and to all creation later when the first humans (by the prompting of the serpent) disobeyed God and ate of the Tree of the Knowledge of Good and Evil. Which begs the question, where did the serpent come from, and what was it?

Scripture doesn't enlighten us about the serpent, but theologians speculate that the serpent was actually Lucifer, the fallen angel who, it is thought, was created by God when He created heaven (Rev. 20:2). So maybe there was evil before Adam and Eve disobeyed God, but it had not yet infected humanity or the earthly creation.

That being said, when did creation start? Scripture says that according to God's time, there were six days between the beginning of

His creation and the creation of the first humans (Gen. 1:26–31). We have visual evidence from the Hubble telescope that there are objects in our universe that are at least 13.4 billion years old, and scientists estimate that the universe is actually at least 13.8 billion years old.[1] Based on the concept that God's time and our time can be different, this doesn't pose a problem for me. I'll go with the 13.8 billion number in our time scale.

Well then, when were the first humans created? While the Bible is not specific about when Adam and Eve would have existed, some biblical scholars have calculated from biblical genealogies and recorded history that it was approximately 6 thousand years ago.[2]

On the other hand, scientists, through genetics and anthropological study, have determined that even though our early *Homo erectus* ancestors had been developing for at least a million years, there was a mitochondrial Eve that lived somewhere around 200,000

---

[1] Mark Prigg for Dailymail,.com, Pub. 13:21EST, 3 March 2016

[2] Lita Cosner, "How Dose the Bible Teach 6000 Years," by Lita Cosner, https//creation.com/6000-years

years ago, who is the common ancestor of all living humanity.[3] As the Bible is not specific on this point, I tend to lean toward the scientific determination.

The questions that faced me at this point were as follows: Did this most recent human common ancestor of ours who came into being (was created) 200,000 years ago have at that time, what separates us from all the other animals and other hominids, and is it evident in our DNA today? Or is it what we call a soul that might have come later when human consciousness developed? And finally, was God involved?

DNA analysis of humans and chimpanzees (our most recent nonhuman common ancestor) shows that our genetic makeups are nearly 99 percent alike.[4] However, in 2006, Katherine Pollard and her colleagues at the University of California, by using a newly developed computer program, were able to identify the first 202 HARs. HARs (human accelerated regions)

---

[3] Mitocondrial Eve, "mMain aArticle: "Macro-haplogroup L (mtDNA)." Wikipedia.

[4] Smithsonian Institution, National Museum of Natural History, Genetic Evidence, DNA, humanorigins.si.edu, Nov. 14, 2017

are sequences of DNA that have been conserved essentially unchanged over millions of years in other animals but have changed rapidly in humans since we evolved from our common ancestors, the chimpanzees. Identified HARs now include nearly 3,000 genome sequences. Researchers have come a long way toward understanding HARs and their roles in human evolution but are still far from understanding their specific functions. However, several of the HARs encompass genes known to produce proteins important to neurodevelopment. Researchers feel that it is likely that most of the HARs will be found to have vital roles in what sets us apart from other higher primates.[5]

One has to ask the question: why did these DNA segments suddenly (in genetic terms) start to change relatively rapidly, and then only in humans, after hundreds of millions of years of showing practically no change at all in other animal DNA? To me, until science can prove otherwise, this has the fingerprints of God all over it. It also seems logical that since all her

---

[5] Katherine S. Pollard, "Decoding Human Accelerated Regions," *The scientist*, August 1, 2016, the-scientist.com

descendants have HARs, our mitochondrial Eve must have had them as well.

———————

Now, this brings me back to my original questions about evil. Genesis tells us that sometime after Adam and Eve were created, there was the well-known episode concerning the Tree of the Knowledge of Good and Evil. It was at that point that humans received the ability to understand, and to know the difference between, good and evil. I had to ask, is there anything that science has discovered that could correspond with this biblical event?

By about 10,000 years ago, the first stirrings of urban life had begun. Jericho is one of the earliest settlements known and, at that time, occupied an area of about ten acres near the Jordan river and a clear water oasis that shows evidence of numerous previous human settlings.[6] It seems to me that it would be necessary for these early settlements to have had

---

[6]   R. A. Guisepi, ed. "The first towns: Seedbeds of Civilization," *The Origins Of Civilizations*, history-world.org

at least a rudimentary set of rules of social conduct to be able to conduct trade and barter and live together successfully. This then would require the understanding that there are good (acceptable) actions and bad (unacceptable) actions—good and evil, if you will. This being accepted, the knowledge of good and evil must have come to humans sometime after our mitochondrial Eve (200,000 years ago) but before the earliest human communities (10,000 years ago). It also appears that being human and having the ability to comprehend the concept of good and evil are inseparable and are likely related to HARs.

Now, has science discovered any evidence of a Tree of the Knowledge of Good and Evil–type of event in the time period between 10,000 and 200,000 years ago? Well, maybe. If we look at the behavior of our very early ancestors (7 million years ago) in the archaeological record, we can scarcely distinguish it from that of the much later sapiens (humans) 200,000 years ago. That continued to be true until somewhere between 50,000 and 70,000 years ago. At that time, we saw a major event that anthropologists call "the Human Revolution"[7]—a term that denotes a spectacular and relatively sudden (apparently revolutionary) emergence of language, consciousness, and culture in our species.

Chris Knight, professor of anthropology, puts it this way: "Everything distinctively human about our nature; our ability to speak, to see ourselves as others see us, to aspire to act on moral principle; has come to prevail in our species thanks precisely to the greatest revolution in history."[8]

Although there is a great deal of opposition, some scientists, faced with the absence of a more plausible explanation, come very close to suggesting that there might be "creationistic" forces involved. Until there is a more plausible explanation, that's where I go. But I'm willing to call it God.

---

[7] "The Human Revolution (human origins)," Wikipedia, en.m.wikipedia.org

[8] Chris Knight, "The Human Revolution," chrisknight. co.uk

Now this is where sin and evil begin to come in. Before humans had the ability to know the difference between right and wrong (good and evil), how could they choose to do wrong? I don't believe they could. But after they knew they had the free will to choose to do good or to do evil, or what we call "to sin." But what is evil? And where did evil come from?

Well, I had the *when* and *where*. What I needed was the *who* and the *what*. Many Christian theologians interpret the Bible as saying that it is impossible for God to have created evil because God is good, all good, and only good. Therefore, whatever comes out of Him is all good and only good. I like that understanding of God a lot, but then, where did evil come from? Could it be true that there is something in us that is the source of all evil? I hoped not but plunged ahead on my quest.

I began looking back over what the Bible teaches, and what authors I have read, and pastors I have heard have said that might shed some light on this subject. One author I remember reading stated, "I have seen the man I want to be, and I am not him." A pastor whom I asked about the existence of the "devil" answered thoughtfully, "I do believe a devil exists," and then added "and it is I." The apostle Paul lamented in Romans 7:15–18,

> I do not understand what I do. For what I want to do I do not do, but what I hate I do. And if I do what I do not want to do, I agree that the law is good. As it is, it is no longer I myself who do it, but it is sin living in me. For I know that good itself does not dwell in me, that is, in my sinful nature.

All these sources seem to say that there is something within each of us that is the source of evil in the world, something that keeps us from reaching our potential as human beings. Where I began to find answers was, surprisingly, not only in theology, archaeology, and anthropology but in psychology as well. Archaeology and anthropology make it clear that for over 100 million years prior to the awakening of human consciousness, our genetic ancestors, living in a very dangerous and unforgiving environment, had been acquiring the basic instincts that were necessary for survival. These primordial instincts are centered around survival and reproduction and are our most powerful psychological drives. They are all self-centered, self-serving, impulsive, illogical, and irrational; and they demand immediate satisfaction. And more bad news: we inherit them at birth, and they are hardwired into us in what Sigmund Freud calls the "id."[9] The good news is that at about three years of age, our psyche begins to incorporate counteracting values and morals that we learn from our parents and others. Freud suggests that these values and moral concepts are stored in what he calls the "superego."[10] It is my belief that a lot of these values and concepts, while being communicated to us by our parents, teachers, preachers, and others, surely contain a great deal of the concepts that God values, even though they may have been filtered through any number of human sieves in the process. I believe that it was the incorpo-

---

[9] Saul McLeod, "Id, Ego and Superego," *Simply Psychology*, Published 2007, updated 2016, simplypsychology.org
[10] Ibid

ration of Christian values and morals into our superegos, or into our minds, that Paul was trying to describe in Romans 12:2.

> Do not conform any longer to the pattern of this world, but be transformed by the renewing of your mind. Then you will be able to test and approve what God's will is—his good, pleasing and perfect will.

I believe it is also possible that we received some of these *good* motivations firsthand. If in fact we got them from our parents, where did our parents get them? If it was from their parents, where did they get them? And so on. The thought occurred to me: all human cultures, no matter how primitive, have an understanding of right and wrong. That understanding is most certainly framed by their culture and communicated from generation to generation, but where did it come from? I suspect that it came along with the Tree of the Knowledge of Good and Evil event that happened some 50,000 years ago. How could our ancestors have understood the difference between good and evil if they didn't have at least a rudimental understanding of what was good as well as what was bad? This is further evidenced by the fact that archeologists have discovered that in that brutal and violent prehistoric time, people cared for those who were injured and disabled.[11] It makes me feel closer to God to think that maybe a little bit of his DNA is in all of us. And maybe Freud was wrong. Maybe we are more than only those base instincts that are stored in our id when we are first born. It turns out that tests show that empathy exists in babies. In some recent work Felix Warneken and Michael Tomasello set up a clever experiment where they put toddlers in situations where nobody was looking at them, then an adult would come in and have some sort of minor crisis, such as reaching for something and being unable to get it. Warneken and Tomasello found that toddlers, more often than not, would spontaneously toddle over and try to help.

---

[11] http://www.nytimes.com/2012/12/18/science/ancient-bones-that-tell-a-story-of-compassion.ht

Other studies show that even very young babies will respond by crying when they hear other babies cry, and when they are old enough to move their bodies around, they'll try to comfort the crying baby by stroking them or they'll try to hand over a toy or a bottle.[12] It brings me comfort to believe that we are created more in the image of God than Freud's hypothesis would suggest.

———

So here's the human dilemma as I see it: I, my "self," or "ego," or whatever you want to call it, am sitting here between some very potent, wired-in, and what could be considered evil instincts on one hand, and (if I hope to have any chance at living a decent life) a set of values and morals, mostly authored by God, on the other. My job is to decide which of these opposing forces I will follow in every decision I make, day in and day out 24/7, 365 days a year. How's that for a job description?

---

[12] Paul Bloom, "A New Science of Morality, part 5," 9.17.10 https://www.edge.org/conversation/paul_bloom

The situation suggests to me that it's in the *decision-making* process that humans have the potential for sin. Sin is usually defined something like, "a willful or deliberate violation of some religious or moral principle," or in a religious context, sin is the act of transgression against God or divine law. So at this point, I must conclude that if I, in a decision-making situation, abandon what I recognize as right values and principles and give in to the demands of my baser instincts, I have committed (in religious terms) a sin.

But that still leaves me up in the air concerning evil. Is the id (our inherited instincts, or maybe just the bad ones) the source of evil? Were they always evil, or did they become evil in the Tree of the Knowledge of Good and Evil incident? Or are they simply the survival instincts we inherited from our early ancestors, no more or less evil than the survival instincts of other animals?

Based on my understanding of God as good, all good, and only good, it is very hard for me to believe that God created anything that was evil. Therefore, I tend to believe that no part of us was created evil. I don't believe that there was a change in our instincts caused by a

Tree of the Knowledge of Good and Evil event of some kind. But I do believe that as human consciousness developed, our awareness of right values and morals could have led us to believe that many of our primordial instincts are evil.

Add to this the belief that there could be a fallen angel, Satan, and/or his demons, influencing us at the time of a decision, either directly or by energizing our base instincts. Or maybe there is a Satan, not of God's creation but of ours. Maybe the evils humans have been guilty of over the millennia form an ever-growing body of knowledge that subconsciously influences all humans by stimulating our baser instincts or by numbing our sensitivities. *"It can't be so bad to kill this one person. It happens all the time. Besides, look what Hitler did."*

The possibilities get so tangled I don't know what the right answer is, or if there is a right answer. But this I know: there is a strong force (or forces) that tries to influence my decision making by turning me away from God (right values and morals). I am stuck with that force as part of my reality, and I must be continually on guard against it.

———•••———

Whether we believe these forces to be evil driven or inherited animal instincts, they tend to be invisible. I believe the evil that we see in the world around us is the action taken, or the consequences of the action taken, as a result of sinful decisions. This is the evil that tears at our hearts and leaves us disgusted, angry, and hor-rified. I believe this is the true face of evil. All of this is pulling me toward the conclusion that sin is not so much driven by evil but that evil is the consequence of sin.

Now, I know that not all sinful decisions produce catastrophic consequences, not all bad decisions are sinful, and even decisions made with the best intentions can have unwanted consequences. But in the midst of all that uncer-tainty, here is what my heart tells me:

❖ As long as my intentions are to do good.
❖ As long as my focus is on Christ's teachings.
❖ As long as I respond in good faith to the question, "What is the loving thing to do?"

I have done the best that is *humanly* possible. With that, I can be at peace.

———◆———

When I got to this point, I felt a sense of "Done." So as Christmas approached, I began tidying up my writing and adding the introductory portions and the references to make it complete. But by that time, it had become more and more apparent to me that if I was going to have a clear understanding of my beliefs about the nature of evil, and really bring my writing to completion, there were other, more fundamental theological issues that I needed to be solid on, and it seemed that the place to begin was at the beginning. So it was back to my investigation.

THE BASICS

I can't remember ever not having faith that there is a God, but for me, for a faith to become a sustainable belief there has to be evidence—evidence enough to make that faith believable. The discoveries of science, instead of pulling me away from a belief in God, have provided very strong evidence that God does exist. Robert Jastrow, the founder of NASA's Institute of Space studies, puts it this way:

> Astronomers now find they have painted themselves into a corner because they have proven, by their own methods, that the world began abruptly in an act of creation to which you can trace the seeds of every star, every planet, every living thing in this cosmos and on the earth. And they have found

that all this happened as a product of forces they cannot hope to discover… That there are, what I or anyone would call supernatural forces at work, is now, I think, a scientifically proven fact.

Then I had to consider this: what is the probability that life started and developed out of sheer random chance? Douglas Axe of Cambridge University and author of *Undeniable: How Biology Confirms Our Intuition That Life Is Designed* calculated that the odds of creating a single protein molecule purely by chance are 1 in 10 to the 164th power—a number so large that it is almost imponderable. It has also been calculated that even under perfect conditions, with these odds, the process would take much, much longer than the 15 billion years that the universe has been in existence to produce that one protein molecule.[13]

---

[13] "What are the Odds," https://www.str.blog/building-a-protein-by-Chance #.WUQrsty1u01

And then add this: at the moment of conception, a fertilized human egg contains all the information necessary to build an adult human being. One cell contains the information that will direct each ensuing developing cell exactly when and how to develop. That's an immense amount of information.

I wonder what the odds are of that kind of complexity developing spontaneously out of chaos. There are many more arguments that promote the existence of God, but these alone contain enough evidence to solidify my belief that God exists, and He was the cause of creation.

———•••———

All of the evidence of God's active involvement in humanity that I had investigated to this point had been in the ancient past. Was there evidence of God's ongoing involvement with us?

Well, as recently (at least in geological terms) as a little over 2,000 years ago, scripture tells us that God is so involved with us and loves us so that he sent his only son, Jesus, to save us from our sins through his death and resurrection. Skeptics say, "Impossible." But who would be better equipped to know if Jesus was who he said he was than his original apostles? Almost all His original apostles died a martyr's death. Lee Strobel, the author of *The Case for Christ*, makes the point that "though people will die defending their beliefs, people will not die for their religious beliefs if they know that their religious beliefs are false." Those original apostles were certainly in a position to know the truth about *who* and *what* Jesus was. The fact that all but John died defending that truth is strong evidence that the Jesus story is accurate.

There is much more in Lee Strobel's book that provides very strong evidence of the veracity of the biblical account of Jesus's life, death, and resurrection; but there are many others as well. One such source is Stan Telchin, a successful Jewish businessman and the author of *Betrayed*, who attempted to debunk the idea that Jesus was the Messiah by finding all the Old Testament prophesies concerning the expected Messiah and applying them to Jesus. He then asked a statistician to calculate the odds that one person would fit that description. After completing his task and realizing that the number was of such a magnitude as to be inconceivable in standard mathematical terms, the statistician put his findings this way: "If you covered the whole state of Texas with silver dollars, one foot deep, and on the back of one of them was a big red X, your chance of picking up that one coin would be greater." The evidence that Telchin discovered in his investigation convinced him to become a believer. I am convinced by the arguments provided by Strobel and Telchin, and many other sources as well, that Jesus is neither a lunatic nor a liar or worse (as some say), but is exactly who he said he is.

What about now? Well, there are thousands, maybe millions, of people living today who are absolutely convinced that God has intervened in their lives. Their stories are everywhere. On the other hand, there are probably just as many people who say that these accounts are all delusional in some way.

I understand both sides of the argument and have been on both sides at different times in my life. However, at this point in my life, I believe that God does intervene in our lives. I don't understand why or how God chooses to, or not to—I just know there is enough evidence to lead me to believe that on occasion, He does. Here are a couple of experiences that pretty much seal the deal for me.

Bill Henderson, one of my close friends and a spiritual companion, is a PhD physical chemist, cancer researcher, university professor emeritus, and an avid fly fisherman. He related the following experience to me this way:

> I was trout fishing alone on a small stream. It was early in the season. No one else had ventured out, at least not to this secluded spot. I had fished one side of the stream and decided to find a shallow place where I could wade across the stream and fish the other side. I had not estimated well how cold the water was or how that cold would affect my body (not so young anymore).

Somewhere about midstream, I realized that my legs were getting numb and were cramping up. Before I could respond, my legs gave way, and I was washed downstream to a place that was shallow enough that I could hold on to some rocks and keep my head out of the water. I realized that I was in a desperate situation. My legs were useless, and my arms would soon go the same way.

That time came. As I began to lose my grip on the rocks, I could see no way out for me, so I said, "Well, God, I guess this is it." And I let go.

The next thing I remember was like an out-of-body experience. I was above the stream, and I could see my body being dragged from the water by something unseen. And then, I don't know how much later, I found myself lying facedown on the bank of the stream with my cheek resting on my hands. I remember that distinctly because I could raise my head just enough to see my wristwatch. It was a full half hour before I had recovered enough to begin to make my way, very slowly, back to my car. There was no one around when I fell into the water, and there was no one there when I came to on the bank; and if God had not stepped in to save me, I would have died that day.

Most of the opponents of out-of-body experiences claim that they are manifestations of a malfunctioning brain due to overwhelming stress, injury, lack of oxygen, or other near-death conditions. That might explain the neurological part, but not the physical part. How did Bill get out of the river and onto the bank without the use of his arms and legs? Certainly, Bill's education and experience in the medical field would have allowed him to make an accurate assessment of his medical condition at the time. And there is no reason to think that a man of Bill's reputation and character would fabricate such a story.

As I write this, I have to pause. One of the major elements of my discernment process has been my personal experience. Yet for some reason, I hesitate to include here an experience of my own. Maybe it's because I don't want to seem holier-than-thou, or favored by God, or something like that. But I risk its inclusion in the hope that it will be helpful to those who may read this writing. So here goes.

In a guided meditation, our retreat group was invited to go along with the apostles into the upper room for the last supper with Jesus. Our guide described the street scene. In my mind, I could see the steps going up the outside of the building that housed the upper room. As we approached and started up the stairs, I noticed that the apostles disappeared one by one until I was alone as I climbed.

At the top of the stairs, the afternoon sun shone brightly over the building's roof into my eyes as I peered through an open door into total darkness. Our guide was continuing the meditation, describing the room in detail, but I could see nothing but black. I ventured into the darkness, one step across the threshold. There was nothing but darkness. In my mind, I went back out the door and tried it again, then again, and again, meanwhile losing all awareness of our guide's words. I don't know how long I tried, but at some point, our guide's words began seeping into my consciousness saying that our session was over and inviting us to revisit that meditation in our free time before the next teaching session.

So I found a quiet place, sat down, and tried over and over to go into that room and see what was there. I could see nothing but black. I tried everything I could think of. I remember thinking at one point, *This is my meditation. I'll just go out to my pickup truck* [where that came from, I don't know] *and get my generator and work lights and set them up here in the room.* So in my mind I went down the stairs, got my generator and lights from my truck, lugged them up the stairs, hooked them up, and turned them on. I couldn't believe it. The darkness was so pervasive that it sucked up every bit of the light. The room was still completely dark. When I looked at the lights, all I could see was a faint orange glow from the bulbs. (The Lord moves in mysterious ways.)

Finally, I had to give up and head back to the next session. As I put my hand on the handrail of the stairs leading back to the classroom, a vision of that dark room flashed into my mind. But this time, in one corner, and the only thing visible, was a figure (that I recognized as Jesus) sitting on a pillow. I decided to find a place to sit down and see what would happen.

As soon as I sat down, I was back, standing just inside the door of that dark room. Jesus got up and came across the room. He stood directly in front of me and said to me, *"It's enough that you came and sought me."* Then he was gone, and the room was still dark.

I've never seen what was in that room. But in that moment, I knew that what He meant was that I would not always be successful in my attempts to be all that God intended me to be, but that was okay. As long as I was seeking Him and trying to do the best that I could, that would be enough. God's grace would cover the rest.

As I have thought about this experience over the years since, it seems more than a little interesting that as precisely as I knew the words He spoke to me, I never heard his voice. And as closely as we stood together, I can't remember seeing his face.

But what a gift! I have come to know, with profound assurance, that God is always watching over us; and sometimes He reaches into our world with great love and compassion.

———•••———

In an effort to be thorough in the investigation of my belief system, I had to ask myself if there were other things that I say I believe but that perhaps needed more examination. The Apostle's Creed came quickly to mind. The creed that as a Christian I had professed many times and what I thought contained the nonnegotiable elements of Christian beliefs. Had I ever really thought about whether I believed everything it said or implied? Well, no. Then I wondered, *How could that have happened?* I guess I had reasoned that if this is the creed we say at church, it must be what Christians believe. Over the years, however, I had come to realize that, that wasn't what every Christian believed. It wasn't even what every member of my church believed. But somehow that revelation hadn't sunk in to the extent that I had thought much about it. Well, this was the time.

THE CREED

Apostle's Creed

I believe in God, the Father almighty,
creator of heaven and earth.

I believe in Jesus Christ, God's
only Son, our Lord,
who was conceived by the Holy Spirit,
born of the Virgin Mary,
suffered under Pontius Pilate,
was crucified, died, and was buried;
he descended to the dead.
On the third day he rose again;
he ascended into heaven,
he is seated at the right hand of the Father,
and he will come to judge the living and the dead.

I believe in the Holy Spirit,
the holy catholic Church,
the communion of saints,
the forgiveness of sins,
the resurrection of the body,
and the life everlasting. Amen.

Apostle's Creed

Church of England,
Book of Common Prayer

I believe in God the Father Almighty,
Maker of heaven and earth:
And in Jesus Christ his only Son our Lord,

Who was conceived by the Holy Ghost,
Born of the Virgin Mary,
Suffered under Pontius Pilate,
Was crucified, dead, and buried:
He descended into hell;
The third day he rose again from the dead;
He ascended into heaven,
And sitteth on the right hand of
God the Father Almighty;
From thence he shall come to judge
the quick and the dead.

I believe in the Holy Ghost;
The holy Catholick Church;
The Communion of Saints;
The Forgiveness of sins;
The Resurrection of the body,
And the Life everlasting.
Amen.

The Nicene Creed

I believe in one God, the Father almighty,
maker of heaven and earth,
of all things visible and invisible.
I believe in one Lord Jesus Christ,
the Only Begotten Son of God,
born of the Father before all ages.
God from God, Light from Light,
true God from true God,
begotten, not made, consubstantial with the Father;
through him all things were made.
For us men and for our salvation
he came down from heaven,
and by the Holy Spirit was incarnate of the Virgin Mary,
and became man.
For our sake he was crucified under Pontius Pilate,
he suffered death and was buried,
and rose again on the third day
in accordance with the Scriptures.
He ascended into heaven
and is seated at the right hand of the Father.
He will come again in glory
to judge the living and the dead
and his kingdom will have no end.
I believe in the Holy Spirit, the Lord, the giver of
life who proceeds from the Father and the Son,
who with the Father and the Son is adored and glorified,
who has spoken through the prophets.
I believe in one, holy, catholic and apostolic Church.
I confess one Baptism for the forgiveness of sins
and I look forward to the resurrection of the dead.

As I began investigating, the diversity of the subject soon became evident. My own church hymnal contained not one but three creeds and seven other affirmations of faith. Further investigation turned up over 160 creeds and affirmations of faith.[14] As I looked these over, it was easy to see the many commonalities they contained, but there were also significant differences.

I had already come to terms with my beliefs concerning God the Creator and God the Son, and I am willing to accept the existence of God the Holy Spirit on faith. Therefore, the concept of the Trinitarian nature of God seems comfortable, based on the evidence contained in scripture and in numerous time-honored Christian church traditions.

The remainder of the assertions of the creeds includes the concepts of the universality of the church, the communion of saints, the forgiveness of sins, the resurrection of the body, and the life everlasting. Each of these has a number of equally plausible understandings that have been expressed in the writings of persons of many faith traditions over many centuries. These concepts

---

[14] https://en.wikipedia.org/wiki/List_of_Christian_creeds

continue to be earnestly debated and I believe are best understood in the context of one's personal understandings and beliefs as the Holy Spirit leads each of us. But, here are some thoughts

The catholic (universal) church

The catholic (universal) church is most often thought of as one worldwide church composed of many denominations, sort of a church of churches. But that concept does not give me much solace as the presence of denominations has always felt divisive to me. What warms my heart is being able to sense, to feel the presence of millions of individual Christian souls surrounding me in the loving embrace of the Body of Christ. That's what I see as the church universal. I don't know how else to explain it.

The communion of saints

The communion of saints adds to our vision of the Body of Christ the understanding that it is not only the union of the living members of the church universal but that it also includes those members who have died. This understanding speaks to the belief that there is a mystical bond uniting both the living and the dead. For me, this not only enhances my understanding of the Body of Christ, it fosters a sense of presence— the presence of my family and friends who have passed on—when I take communion.

The forgiveness of sins

A friend recently asked me, "Who was the most sinful person who ever died?" In the absence of a response from me, my friend offered, "Jesus." The reasoning was that when Jesus died, he had taken on all the sins of humanity and therefore had to be the most sin-filled person to have ever died.

When I have repeated the line in the Apostle's Creed that expresses my belief in "the forgiveness of sins," I have always associated it with Jesus's dying on the cross for the sins of all mankind. And even though I somehow understood that my sins were included, it was a long time before I came to understand that it included all the sins ever to be committed by all the people who would ever live, whether they were saved Christians or not. For me, that puts this already-unimaginable act of love in a whole new light.

But there's more. I have come to understand that if I say that I believe in the forgiveness of sins, I am called to forgive all those who have sinned, or ever will sin, against me. That adds a whole new significance to my affirmation.

The afterlife

There are various understandings of what happens in our afterlife. The various creeds agree (with some variations) that there is some kind of resurrection that leads to an eternal existence but disagree on where we go when we die and how long we stay there.

The *where* disagreement shows up in the assertion of where Jesus went immediately after his death. The Apostle's Creed indicates that He "descended to the dead." The Nicene Creed makes no mention of where He went. Other creeds say He went to hell. The Bible indicates in Luke 23:43 that when Jesus died, He went to *paradise.*

Now, I grew up with the understanding that when we died, if we were good enough, we would go directly to heaven, and that paradise and heaven were the same place. It never occurred to me that there could be a different interpretation of what happened to us after we died.

But as I got older, it started to seem incongruous to me that the dead would go to heaven or hell immediately after the death event, only to be removed for the final judgment, and then maybe, or maybe not, returned. It didn't seem to me that a loving God would give a soul a taste of heaven and then take it away, or that he would allow a soul to languish in hell for some undetermined length of time before ultimately being accepted into heaven. (Of course, this is assuming that time has some relevance in the "dead" state.)

It wasn't until recent years that I began to identify information that suggested that there was a concept of an intermediate state of being between death and judgment that was widely known and ancient in origin. Where had I been? Death, then go directly to heaven, "do not pass Go," had been such an indelible part of my belief system that I hadn't even thought to ask the question, is there another possibility?

I did some research. I became aware, belatedly, that there is a widely held view that dates at least back to the second century. This view holds that there is an intermediate state of existence between death and judgment. This existence is said to take place in Hades, the place of the dead, not to be confused with hell. Hades is divided into two sides—the good side, paradise (not to be confused with heaven), and Gehenna, the bad side (again, not hell). Who knew? Apparently a lot of people. This concept opens up a lot of questions like, Are the souls in Hades conscious or unconscious? Are they aware of time? Are the ones in Gehenna redeemable?

Some would say, "It is what it is. It doesn't even matter." Well, I think it does matter. I don't believe it is likely that many of us will die in a perfectly sinless state, and globally there are many who will die, or have died, without the acceptance, or even the knowledge, of Jesus Christ. If there is an intermediate existence for us after our death and before our final judgment wherein our spiritual being is conscious and communicable, it would fit my understanding that a God of unconditional love will do anything short of overriding our freedom of will to bring us to the sort of relationship that God wishes for us all. And that He would work actively for that relationship, right up to the moment of final judgment.

This concept of postmortem evangelism is rigorously contested, and not everyone thinks it's a good idea. One of the main objections seems to be that in the light of an understanding that

God will work for our salvation after our death, what would be the impetus for anyone to live a decent life? We'll just have a high old time in this life and let God fix us up after we're dead.

Well, I understand their point. But here's a thought: There are consequences to every decision. Every week, Connie and I sit down with other members of our church and pray over the prayer requests that have been sent in to our church. We have seen over and over again the length and breadth of suffering that we humans endure in this earthly life. We have often said, "How do people who don't have God to turn to make it through these kinds of devastating calamities?" So here's the question I have to ask: Believing in postmortem evangelism, would I then give up the assurance of God's marvelous grace and healing love and face a lifetime of possible hellish tragedies without his aid and strength, just so I could embark on a corrupt lifestyle here on earth? I don't believe I could make that trade-off. I wonder how many people would.

There are many other arguments against postmortem evangelism. I have chosen the synopsis of a feature article written by Ronald H.

Nash of the Christian Research Institute as rep-
resentative of the more common arguments
presented by theologians opposing this view.

SYNOPSIS

by Ronald H. Nash

The view that belief in Jesus is necessary for salvation is known as *exclusivism*. It should be noted, however, that some exclusivists contend that those who do not believe the gospel during their earthly lives will be given an opportunity to believe the gospel after they die and so be saved. This view is known as *postmortem evangelism* (PME).

One well-known advocate of PME, Gabriel Fackre, argues that Scripture teaches that each human's destiny is *not* fixed at death. The context of several key Bible passages, however, does not support his interpretation. In fact, these passages clearly say that everyone will die and be judged (Heb. 9:27) and that each person's eternal destiny, either reward or condemnation, will be based on what was done in this life (Matt. 7:21–23; 13:36–43; John 5:28–29). Jesus, moreover, taught that each human's destiny is fixed at death; for example, in His story of Lazarus, who was eternally in paradise, and the rich man, who was eternally in torment (Luke 16:19–31). Finally, the description of the great white throne judgment in Revelation 20:11–15 unquestionably indicates that our eternal destiny is based on our earthly life. In these and other passages, physical death marks the boundary of human opportunity to be saved. Belief in PME, meanwhile, has serious negative implications for Christian evangelism and missions. The weakness of PME arguments and the total silence of Scripture regarding opportunities to hear the gospel after death, therefore, should cause Christians to reject this view.

I will not enter into an argument with Mr. Nash's views. However, by my reading, the referenced scriptural passages do not specifically preclude postmortem evangelism. Take a look and see what you think.

The scriptures cited by Mr. Nash seem to me to teach that our salvation is only through our earthly works and has little or nothing to do with God's grace. And therefore, there can be no postmortem evangelism. This poses a dilemma for me. My overarching understanding of scripture is that God is Love and He loves all humanity, as underserving as they may be, with an unconditional love. This understanding is leading me to believe that postmortem evangelism is at least possible.

I also believe that there is other scriptural evidence that leaves this possibility open. I considered these:

Ephesians 2:8-9

For by grace you have been saved through faith. And this is not your own doing; it is the gift of God, not a result of works, so that no one may boast.

Romans 8:38-39

For I am convinced that neither death nor life, neither angels nor demons, neither the present nor the future, nor any powers, neither height nor depth, nor anything else in all creation, will be able to separate us from the love of God that is in Christ Jesus our Lord.

1 Peter 3:18-20
Jesus went to Sheol and proclaimed to the spirits

Matthew 28:20
Jesus promised he will be with us always, to the very end of the age."

2 Peter 3:9
The Lord is patient toward us, not wishing that any should perish, but that all should reach repentance.

Romans 14:11
It is written: "'As surely as I live,' says the Lord, 'every knee will bow before me; every tongue will acknowledge God.'"

Philippians 2:10
So that at the name of Jesus every knee should bow, in heaven and on earth and under the earth.

So my problem is not with the opponents of postmortem evangelism. My problem is that I am confronted with seemingly conflicting scriptural teachings. If I believe that my final judgment will be based on earthly works, then I must abandon salvation by God's grace, and I must give up a belief that God loves me so much that he will pursue my sanctification and eventual salvation to the very last day. At this point, I do not have the evidence that makes me willing to give up either of these beliefs.

As I come to this understanding, there are tears falling on my keyboard. There is joy and peace involved, and now I know why.

I also know that my perceived conflict of scripture is only temporary. I have been here before, and the problem has always been the existence of a hole in my understanding of scripture, not scripture itself. I trust that, sooner or later, God will give me the grace to resolve the dilemma.

No matter how all of this works, there is an almost universal expectation that after death, there is some sort of resurrection and eternal existence. However, the concept of the resurrection is shrouded in the controversy of what is meant by the word "body" when used in relation to our resurrection. Is the "body" physical or spiritual? If it's physical, does it have spiritual properties? If it's spiritual, does it have physical properties? If it's physical, is it our original body, or is it a new version? If it's spiritual, will it retain our earthly identity? Here again, we could ask, does it even matter to us in this earthly life? In this case, I think it probably doesn't. And as my mother would say when we had this kind of family discussion about heaven, "I think we are all going to be surprised when we get there."

OTHER PONDERABLES

One of the questions that I hear often asked is, "What does a person have to do to be a Christian?" There are any number of beliefs about what it takes to be considered a Christian. There may be more, but the following is a cumulative list of the requirements of various Christian denominations that I was able to come up with.

One must do the following:

Confess one's sins, and ask for God's Forgiveness
Believe that Jesus is the Son of God
Believe that Jesus is their Savior and died for the forgiveness of their sins
Believe that Jesus is resurrected from the dead
Believe that Jesus ascended into heaven
Find community with other Christians
Be baptized
Love Jesus and others

Read the Bible as much as possible
Resolve to follow Jesus as Lord (walk in the Spirit)

It is easy for me to believe that anyone doing all of the above requirements would be considered a Christian. However, while each of the sources I researched had some combination of some of the elements on the list, none required all the actions on the list to be satisfied.

It appears to me that there is no definitive answer as to what one must do to be a Christian. It also seems to me that a much more important question is, "What do I, as a Christian, need to do to be saved?"

The same list began to emerge as I researched the answer. Scripture again provided Ephesians 2:8–9.

> For by grace you have been saved through faith. And this is not your own doing; it is the gift of God, not a result of works, so that no one may boast.

If I apply this understanding to the list assembled from the various faith traditions and remove those items that require one's own doing, it leaves us with the requirement that one must believe the following:

Jesus is the son of God.
Jesus is my savior.
Jesus died for the forgiveness of my sins.
Jesus is resurrected from the dead.
Jesus ascended into heaven.

Is that it? It sounds good, but I am haunted by the scripture in James 2:17 that says,

Thus also faith by itself, if it does not have works, is dead.

When I compare that with Ephesians 2:8–9,

For by grace you have been saved through faith. And this is not your own doing; it is the gift of God, not a result of works, so that no one may boast.

it seems that I am confronted with another case of apparently conflicting scriptures. However, in this case, scripture provides what is for me a resolution of the incompatibility. Galatians 5:6 says,

> The only thing that counts is faith expressing itself through love.

This scripture confirms that faith is the necessary element of our salvation as presented in Ephesians and at the same time confirms that it is powerless if it does not result in expressions of love (which I would consider the "works" referenced in James). This understanding really fleshes out a paraphrase of 1 Corinthians 13:1–3 that comes from somewhere in my childhood, "All the good works in the world are of no good to you if they are not done out of love." Now I get it.

—————◆————

Up to this point, I had been "all in" on the idea that faith alone was the means of salvation, and maybe you are too. From that perspective, here is the way I look at it.

Some purist naysayers argue that the Ephesian 2:8–9 scripture is not applicable because the mere act of professing a belief is, in fact, one's "own doing." And even if God's grace is 99.99% of salvation, there's still that .01% that is human doing. Well, my understanding of God's grace is big enough to cover that .01%, but here is another thought.

In business school, we were taught that the person with the most information makes the best decisions; and if you have all the information, there is actually no decision to be made. The next step becomes obvious.

I am comfortable with the belief that God is tenacious in the pursuit of our salvation and, through his miraculous grace, will provide each of us with whatever experience, knowledge, or inspiration is needed to bring us to that point where there will no longer be a need for a decision. The obvious next step will be to surrender to God. It will just happen.

Either concept seems plausible to me, but the scriptural evidence seems to be pulling me

toward the former. Either way, I know that we are in God's loving hands.

Prayer is one of the things that I continue to ponder. Even though I feel it so strongly at times, it often gets crowded out of my daily life by the sheer busyness of living. There have been many times that I have struggled with a vexing problem, using every tool in my mental toolbox to no avail. With nothing else to reach for, I find myself saying, "You know, Dave, you could try prayer." Why is it that instead of being the first tool I try, it winds up being the last one? I suspect that it has a lot to do with parental influences and technical training that have formed a high level of self-reliance in me. I find it somewhat uncomfortable to ask for help. But deeper than that, as I have tried to think this through, I have begun to form a suspicion that maybe my problem is that I don't trust prayer enough. That's very hard for me to admit and seems also rather strange as I have seen immediate and compelling results from prayer that, I would think, would foster a more enduring trust.

I was in the prayer chapel at a men's retreat. A gentleman who had been a longtime member of our faith community was scheduled to make a speech to the attendees on that day. This much-loved and much-respected gentleman, being very humble in nature, had declined many invitations to speak over the years but had finally agreed to give a talk to the men on this retreat. He was very nervous and apprehensive when he entered the prayer chapel that day to be prayed over prior to his talk. The community, knowing his great humility and retiring nature, had filled the room to over-flowing to offer their prayers of support and love. You could literally feel the presence of the Holy Spirit in that room as we prayed. The man who rose from the kneeler and walked confidently to the door was a different man than had entered the room that day. He went on to give a flawless and deeply compelling speech and spiritual witness to the men attending that retreat.

Over the years, I have marveled at how sim-ilar that experience was to what I imagine the day of Pentecost must have been like for the apostles. On the one hand, the power of the Holy Spirit was poured into my friend through the prayers from many loving hearts. On the other hand, twelve frightened and unsure apostles received the power of the Holy Spirit from the hand of God. It was the indwelling of the Holy Spirit that empowered both the apostles and my friend to go out with great confidence and conviction to spread the Good News to hungry hearts. But for my friend, I believe it was prayer that moved the hand of God.

So I have to ask the question: why do I find it hard to trust prayer? And maybe it's not so much that I don't trust prayer as it is that I just don't understand how it works. Maybe it's because in my humanness, God's response to prayer seems capricious. Why does God answer some prayers and not others? And there are other questions about prayer that I have wrestled with for years. If God doesn't answer my prayer, is it because I didn't pray right or enough? What does God do with opposing prayers? If I praise God when my prayers are answered the way I hoped, is it fair to give Him the blame when they aren't? Why is it important that we praise God? It can't be that God is so narcissistic that He needs to hear our praise. Does prayer really change God's mind? Why do bad things happen to good people?

I certainly don't have all the answers. Maybe because prayer is so closely tied up with God and the mystery of God, that it is not totally knowable by the human mind. Or maybe it's because the *how* and *when* of God's response is sometimes so different from what we expect or hope for, that we don't recognize it as God's answer. Maybe that's why I ask God to take control of my life but want to keep one hand on the steering wheel? I don't know. But I do know that I have experienced the power of God through prayer, and it is amazing.

Today is May 5, 2018, almost exactly a year since I started this journey. Over these many months, I've received a great deal of encouragement to continue on the journey to see where it takes me. However, I have also been asked, "Why are you doing this? Why are you willing to spend so much time and effort to delve into things you can never know for sure?" For those questions, I have a couple of answers. Interestingly enough, they mostly revolve around prayer.

First, I believe that God likes it. I believe that our relationship with Him is of utmost importance to Him. Like all relationships, it grows if we spend time together, if we get to know more about each other, and if we share with each other.

Secondly, for me, when I'm groping for God in the darkness of my limited understanding, that's when I most often hear him speak. Often when I pray I find myself doing all the talking. But when I am totally engrossed in trying to articulate a belief, I will sometimes hear things coming out of my mouth that I know I did not author, thoughts that I know I had not ever formulated before that moment. I am strongly convinced that the cognitive content of these inspirations, those aha moments, is a gift from God as surely as if I had heard the sound of his voice. For me, those are times of extreme closeness with God that have provided me with some of the most intimate prayer experiences I have ever known. Just now it occurred to me that maybe the largest part of the reason I have tears when I have an aha moment (just like this) is because of the deep emotion evoked by the closeness of God that I sense. All of this solidifies my understanding that prayer is mostly (if not all) about relationship and not so much about convincing God to do something we want him to do. The great majority of the stories I've been told about God's miraculous interventions indicate that they came spontaneously in moments of acute need without the bidding of, or even the time for, human prayers. I'm very sure that God is on top of doing what God does. And that He knows without our asking what needs to be done.

Lastly, just because we can never fully *know* something doesn't mean that it is not worth investigating. Even partial knowledge helps form an understanding of a subject and can lead to a future, more defining understanding. And even if all we can do is eliminate those things that we know are not part of whatever we are investigating, that in itself begins to expose the reality of the thing under scrutiny.

Consider the well-known image on the next page. By taking away what is *not* part of that which we would understand, we begin to see the nature of what remains.

Well, I'm at that point again where I'm getting that "Done" feeling. I know it's not that I think my spiritual journey of inquiry is complete. It will just take on a different form. I'm anxious to see where that will take me.

As I have been writing this, a number of things I hoped to be true have become realized beliefs. One of those things that kind of took me by surprise was that the theory of evolution is not necessarily in opposition to the belief that God is the creator of all life. The evidence I see is drawing me to believe that God is probably the author of evolution and is using it to accomplish his plan for humanity. That thought has caused me to also realize that it's rather presumptuous of us to think that present-day humans are the "end all, be all" of human evolution. We could still be relatively early in the chain of human development.

The second, and the one that brought tears to my eyes, is that unlike the god of the Deists who is believed to have created the world, set it in motion, and then has no interaction with human affairs, the God I know seems to have always been with us and has been intimately involved with major events throughout the development of humanity, and He is with us now. He truly is Emmanuel (God with us).

Well, that's my journey. The route had some surprising turns, and even the place where I ended up was a little unexpected, but very pleasing and a joy to my soul. Maybe you have never taken this journey, or maybe it's been a long time, or maybe you've been on any number of these journeys—it doesn't matter. There's no better time to start, or start again, than right now. Don't be afraid to ask questions or to own your doubts. It's because of the doubts that live in all the things I hope to be true that I continue my search to find spiritual clarity.

Almost certainly any journey of spiritual discovery you undertake will be different than mine. The route on which you will be taken and the place where you will end up, will be uniquely yours. But two things more I believe: By the end of the journey, you will have come to know yourself better. And where you end up will be closer to God.

There are tears in my eyes.

God's blessings.

EPILOGUE

Almost exactly a year from the day I got up from my workbench and walked out of my lab and away from a very compelling electronic design project, I finished the first draft of this book. In the four months since, there has been a lot of reading and rereading, changing, adding, writing and rewriting—all the stuff that makes up the first steps of the editing process. Six days ago, all the editing that I and my beta readers could accomplish was completed, and I submitted a draft of this book to the publisher for review. That day, with things out of my hands, I sat down at my workbench with the system that I abandoned over a year ago. Today that system has been remodified, and rebuilt, and the software has been rewritten to accommodate the changes. The final testing has shown that the new design is working exactly as intended.

What are the odds that a complex multi-discipline electronic system would be redesigned, rebuilt, tested, and operating properly in six days after it had been built, redesigned, and rebuilt twice over a two-year period without success? Oh, did I mention that before the final, six-day redesign the engineer on the project took an unexpected year off to think about God?

I don't know if God was involved in why I couldn't see the solution to my design problems for over two years. But I believe that God at least used that as an opportunity to get my attention. I believe that He "nudged" me away from that all-consuming project. I believe that He provided the vehicle of self-examination and writing to get and hold my attention for a year while our relationship grew and my priorities were being straightened out. I believe that he was either directly or indirectly involved in my suddenly seeing the solution to my engineering problems.

Time may give me a different perspective on these events, but for now, these are the most reasonable conclusions I can come to. And now maybe you and I have the real reason this book came to be written.

ENDNOTES

1   Mark Prigg for Dailymail.com, Pub. 13:21EST, 3 March 2016

2   Lita Cosner, "How Dose the Bible Teach 6000 Years," https//creation.com/6000-years

3   Mitocondrial Eve, main article: "Macro-haplogroup L (mtDNA)," *Wikipedia.*

4   Smithsonian Institution, National Museum of Natural History, Genetic Evidence, DNA, humanorigins.si.edu, Nov. 14, 2017

5   Katherine S. Pollard, "Decoding Human Accelerated Regions," *The scientist,* August 1, 2016, the-scientist.com

6   R. A. Guisepi, ed. "The first towns: Seedbeds of Civilization," *The Origins Of Civilizations,* history-world.org

7   "The Human Revolution (human origins)," *Wikipedia,* en.m.wikipedia.org

8   Chris Knight, "The Human Revolution," chrisknight.co.uk

9   Saul McLeod, "Id, Ego and Superego," *Simply Psychology,* Published 2007, updated 2016, simplypsychology.org

10 Ibid

11   http://www.nytimes.com/2012/12/18/science/ancient-bones-that-tell-a-story-of-compassion.ht

12   Paul Bloom, "A New Science of Morality, part 5," 9.17.10 https://www.edge.org/conversation/paul_bloom

13   "What are the Odds," https://www.str.blog/building-a-protein-by-Chance #.WUQrsty1u01

14   https://en.wikipedia.org/wiki/List_of_Christian_creeds

ABOUT THE AUTHOR

David Senften's call to writing came later in life after a successful career as an electronics engineer, inventor, and entrepreneur. David's call to the study of things spiritual resulted from a string of events that began with a "Walk to Emmaus" retreat and culminated in his completion of the Upper Room's two-year Academy for Spiritual Formation. He and his wife, Connie, are members of the United Methodist Church of the Shepherd in Saint Peters, Missouri, where David is involved in various ministries.